FRYING SOLO

First published in Great Britain in 2025 by
Michael O'Mara Books Limited
9 Lion Yard
Tremadoc Road
London SW4 7NQ

A CIP catalogue record for this book is available from the British Library.

Papers used by Michael O'Mara Books Limited are natural,
recyclable products made from wood grown in sustainable
forests. The manufacturing processes conform to the
environmental regulations of the country of origin.

ISBN: 978-1-78929-735-5 in paperback print format

1 2 3 4 5 6 7 8 9 10

Cover design by Barbara Ward
Photographs by William Shaw
Interior design by Ana Bjezancevic
Typeset by Barbara Ward

Printed and bound in China

www.mombooks.com

FRYING SOLO

65 QUICK AND HEALTHY AIR FRYER RECIPES FOR ONE

DENISE SMART

Michael O'Mara Books Limited

CONTENTS

INTRODUCTION

What is *Frying Solo* all about?

This book is packed with 65 healthy and exciting air fryer recipes, to show that cooking for one does not have to be time-consuming, boring or reliant on ready meals, takeaways and batch cooking. It will inspire even the reluctant cook to get inventive.

The air fryer is the perfect kitchen gadget for cooking solo, saving on the need to heat up a large oven, and is perfect for cooking smaller amounts of food.

Air fryers are affordable, energy efficient, easy to use and have well-balanced time and temperature controls, so produce perfect food that is juicy, crisp and delicious. You'll be surprised what you can make in it and you will see that it is more than just a device for cooking chips and frozen food.

This wonderful collection of easy-to-prepare recipes, many for complete meals, covers every occasion, using easily sourced ingredients, and is guaranteed to make preparing and cooking dishes in your air fryer simple and successful.

From perfect soft-boiled eggs with tender asparagus or crunchy granola for breakfast, to speedy mid-week dinners and your favourite classics, with tender, juicy meat and fish, and perfectly cooked vegan and vegetarian choices, there are so many delicious options to create. There is also no need to worry about Friday night takeaways as there are recipes to show how to make healthier versions of your favourite treats.

SO WHAT IS AN AIR FRYER?

The name is deceptive: it is not a fryer as we know it but it is basically a small oven that can cook food that has a fried effect.

It has a heating element located at the top, enhanced by a powerful fan, which circulates the hot air around the food. Air fryers typically heat up speedily and cook food quickly and evenly.

The recipes in this book have been tested in a 4–5-litre capacity, single-drawer air fryer, enabling complete meals to be cooked, but one with dual drawers will work equally as well too. Like ovens, cooking times may vary slightly between different models, so always read your manufacturer's instructions.

To make your recipes successful, you might need to purchase a few items:

- Small ovenproof dishes, ramekins and metal tins.

- Spray bottles are great for filling with oil so you can lightly spritz food while it's cooking.

- Perforated air-fryer liners or non-stick baking (parchment) paper with pierced holes are very useful (remember to never place in the air fryer without food on top as they can fly into the element and start a fire).

- A pair of tongs for turning the food.

There are a few simple rules for the getting the best from your air fryer:

- Always preheat first, cut vegetables and meat and fish into equal-sized pieces or strips.

- Cook food in a single layer and never overcrowd to allow the air and heat to circulate around the food for even cooking.

- Turn food or shake the basket halfway through according to the instructions in the recipes.

Most importantly, I hope you enjoy cooking the recipes and creating your own healthier variations of your favourite foods. Happy air frying solo!

BREAKFAST & BRUNCH

PORRIDGE OATS WITH NUT BUTTER

Serves: 1
Ready in: 6 minutes

40g (¼ cup) jumbo porridge oats
  (old-fashioned rolled oats)
100ml (⅓ cup) milk
100ml (⅓ cup) boiling water
½ tsp vanilla extract
2 tsp nut butter (almond, cashew
  or peanut)

To serve:
fresh berries, such as raspberries,
  blueberries or strawberries

1. Place the oats in an ovenproof bowl
    and stir in the milk, boiling water and
    vanilla extract.

2. Preheat the air fryer to 180°C (350°F).
    Place the bowl of oats inside and cook
    for 5 minutes. Stir well, then stir in the nut
    butter and cook for a further minute.

3. Serve topped with the fresh berries.

Tip: You can adapt your porridge by stirring
in a little ground cinnamon or a few dark
chocolate chips in place of the nut butter.

SHAKSHUKA

Serves: 1
Ready in: about 20 minutes

½ small red onion, sliced
½ small red pepper, thinly sliced
1 small clove of garlic, crushed
1 tsp olive oil
½ tsp ground cumin
½ tsp ground coriander
½ tsp hot smoked paprika
2 medium-sized tomatoes, diced
1 tsp tomato purée (tomato paste)
salt and freshly ground black pepper
1 medium egg
1 tbsp fresh flat leaf parsley, chopped

To serve:
crusty bread

1. Preheat the air fryer to 180°C (350°F). Place the onions, peppers, garlic and olive oil in an ovenproof dish or cake tin and mix well. Place the dish in the air fryer and cook for 8 minutes, stirring halfway through. Add the spices, stir well and cook for a further minute.

2. Add the tomatoes and tomato purée (tomato paste), season and stir. Return to the air fryer and cook for 2 minutes.

3. Make a well in the centre of the mixture and crack in the egg. Return to the air fryer and cook for a further 5–6 minutes, or until the egg is just set.

4. Sprinkle over the parsley and serve immediately with crusty bread.

SPICED BAKED PLUMS AND GRANOLA

Serves: 1
Ready in: 12 minutes

2 tsp maple syrup
1 tbsp fresh orange juice
¼ tsp ground ginger
1 star anise
2 plums, halved and stoned
2 tbsp plant-based yogurt
2 tbsp nutty granola (see below)

1. Mix together the maple syrup, orange juice, ground ginger and star anise in an ovenproof dish. Add the plum halves, cut-side down, and stir gently to coat, then leave to stand for 5 minutes to allow the flavours to mingle.

2. Preheat the air fryer to 180°C (350°F). Turn over the plums and cook in the air fryer for 6–8 minutes until soft and slightly caramelized.

3. Remove the star anise. Serve the plum halves in a bowl with the juice from the cooking dish and some plant-based yogurt, topped with the nutty granola.

NUTS AND SEEDS GRANOLA

Serves: 2 portions
Ready in: about 15 minutes

Any remaining granola can be stored in an airtight container for 2 weeks.

1 tbsp maple syrup or honey
1 tbsp olive oil
50g (⅓ cup) porridge oats
  (old-fashioned rolled oats)
50g (⅓ cup) mixed nuts, such as
  pecans, almonds and walnuts,
  roughly chopped
25 g (3 tbsp) mixed seeds, such as
  sunflower, pumpkin, linseed
½ tsp ground cinnamon
½ tsp ground ginger

1. Mix together the maple syrup and oil in a bowl. Stir in the oats, nuts, seeds and spices and mix well, to combine.

2. Preheat the air fryer to 150°C (300°F). Spread the granola over an air-fryer liner or a piece of pierced non-stick baking (parchment) paper and flatten with a spoon. Cook for 10–12 minutes until golden.

3. Remove from the air fryer and allow to cool, then break into smaller pieces.

SMOKED HADDOCK KEDGEREE

Serves: 1
Ready in: about 25 minutes

1 tsp sunflower oil
½ small red onion, sliced
1 tsp ginger paste
2 tsp mild curry powder
50g (¼ cup) easy-cook long-grain
   rice, rinsed
125ml (½ cup) hot fish or vegetable
   stock
salt and freshly ground black pepper
1 × 100g (3½ oz) skinless smoked
   haddock fillet or loin, cut into
   2.5cm (1 inch) pieces
1 medium egg, at room temperature
50g (¼ cup) frozen peas
juice of ½ a small lemon
1 tbsp fresh flat leaf parsley, chopped

1. Preheat the air fryer to 180°C (350°F) . Add the oil to a metal cake tin or ovenproof dish and heat in the air fryer for 1 minute. Stir in the onion, ginger paste and curry powder and cook for 2 minutes.

2. Add the rice, stir well, pour over the stock, season and cover tightly with foil. Cook for 10 minutes. Stir well, then add the fish. Re-cover with the foil, then place the egg alongside the tin. Cook for 10 minutes.

3. Remove the egg, then stir the peas into the rice mixture. Re-cover, return to the air fryer and cook for 2 minutes until the rice is tender and the peas are cooked. Leave to stand for 2 minutes. Stir in the lemon juice.

4. Meanwhile, peel the egg and cut into quarters. Transfer the kedgeree to a bowl, add the egg and sprinkle with parsley. Serve immediately.

BANANA AND BLUEBERRY PANCAKES

Serves: 1 – makes 3 pancakes
Ready in: about 12 minutes

1 small, very ripe banana
2 tbsp milk
1 tsp melted butter
½ tsp vanilla extract
50g (¼ cup) plain flour
½ tsp baking powder
1 tsp caster sugar
1 egg white
50g (¼ cup) fresh blueberries, plus a
   few extra to serve
sunflower oil for greasing

To serve:
maple syrup or honey, for drizzling

1. In a jug, mash the banana with a fork, then beat in the milk, melted butter and vanilla extract.

2. Sift the flour into a bowl and stir in the baking powder and sugar. Whisk the egg white in a clean bowl until it forms soft peaks.

3. Stir the banana mixture into the flour with 1 tablespoon of the egg white, to loosen, then gently fold in the remaining egg white to make a batter. Stir in the blueberries.

4. Preheat the air fryer to 180°C (350°F) and place an air-fryer liner or a piece of pierced non-stick baking (parchment) paper brushed with a little oil inside. Spoon heaped tablespoons of the batter mixture onto the liner to make 3 pancakes, leaving a little space between them to spread. Flatten slightly and cook for 5 minutes until the pancakes are golden and the blueberries have burst.

5. Serve with a few extra blueberries, drizzled with maple syrup or honey.

MINI BANANA BREAD

Serves: 1 — makes 1 small loaf
Ready in: 14 minutes

1 tbsp sunflower oil, plus a little extra
  for spritzing
1 small, ripe banana
2 tsp honey or maple syrup
2 tbsp self-raising flour
1 tbsp porridge oats
  (old-fashioned rolled oats)
1 tbsp dried raisins or sultanas
½ tsp ground mixed spice
¼ tsp baking powder

To serve:
fresh fruit and yogurt

1. Lightly spritz a mini metal loaf tin or cardboard loaf tin (about 150ml/2–3 cup capacity) or place a paper muffin case in a small ramekin. Mash the banana in a bowl and stir in the oil and honey or maple syrup. Stir in all the remaining ingredients.

2. Preheat the air fryer to 180°C (350°F). Pour the mixture into the prepared tin and cook in the air fryer for 12–14 minutes, or until a cocktail stick comes out clean. (Cooking time will be shorter if you're using a metal tin.)

3. Allow to cool in the tin or case for 10 minutes.

4. Serve warm or cold with fresh fruit and yogurt if desired.

Tip: If you don't have self-raising flour, simply use regular flour and add 1 tsp of baking powder and an extra ¼ tsp of salt.

BAKED EGGS WITH HAM AND SPINACH

Serves: 1

Ready in: about 10–12 minutes

25g (1 oz) sliced ham

50g (1 ½ cups) baby spinach

1 tbsp crème fraîche

2 tsp Parmesan cheese, freshly grated

freshly ground black pepper

1 egg

To serve:

granary toast

1. Line a ramekin with the ham, to cover the base and sides. Place the spinach in a colander and pour over a kettle of boiling water to wilt. Leave to drain and cool slightly, then squeeze the excess water out of the spinach.

2. Chop the spinach, then place it in a small bowl and stir in the crème fraîche, Parmesan and a grind of black pepper.

3. Preheat the air fryer to 180°C (350°F). Spoon the spinach mixture into the ramekin and break the egg on top. Cook in the air fryer for 8–10 minutes until the white has set and the yolk is still soft.

4. Serve immediately with granary toast.

BREAKFAST TEACAKE

Makes: 2
Ready in: 15 minutes, plus 1 hour soaking time for fruit

25g (¼ cup) dried mixed fruit

25g (¼ cup) dried apricots, chopped
into small pieces

100ml (⅓ cup) hot tea (Earl Grey or
English Breakfast)

1 tbsp sunflower or light olive oil,
plus extra for greasing

1 medium egg

50g (⅓ cup) self-raising flour

¼ tsp ground cinnamon

1 tsp caster sugar

To serve:

jam

1. Place the fruit in a small bowl and pour over the hot tea, leave to stand for 1 hour. Lightly oil 2 × 250ml (1 cup) metal pudding moulds or line 2 ramekins with paper muffin cases.

2. In a jug, whisk together the oil and egg.

3. Place the flour, cinnamon and sugar in a bowl, stir in the fruit and tea mixture and the egg mixture until combined.

4. Preheat the air fryer to 160°C (325°F). Divide the mixture equally between the moulds. Place in the air fryer and cook for 12–14 minutes or until a cocktail stick comes out clean.

5. Allow to cool slightly, then remove from the moulds and cool on a wire rack.

6. Serve warm or cold with a little jam. Store the extra cake in an airtight container for up to 2 days.

SOFT-BOILED EGG WITH PANCETTA-WRAPPED ASPARAGUS

Serves: 1
Ready in: 9 minutes

6 large asparagus spears
3 slices pancetta
1 medium egg, room temperature
freshly ground black pepper

1. Snap the woody ends off the asparagus. Cut the pancetta rashers in half, then gently stretch out each one with the back of a knife.

2. Wrap each asparagus spear in pancetta.

3. Preheat the air fryer to 180°C (350°F). Place the egg, in its shell, in the air fryer and arrange the asparagus around the egg. Cook for 6 minutes, turning the asparagus halfway through until the pancetta is crispy.

4. Transfer the egg to an egg cup and serve with the asparagus for dipping and a grind of black pepper.

MARMALADE FRENCH TOAST

Serves: 1
Ready in: about 12 minutes

1 egg
¼ tsp ground cinnamon
1 tsp caster sugar
1 tsp orange zest, grated (optional)
2 tbsp milk
2 medium slices sourdough bread
2 tbsp orange marmalade
sunflower oil, for spritzing

1. In a shallow dish, whisk together the egg, cinnamon, sugar and orange zest, if using, then whisk in the milk.

2. Spread 1 slice of the bread with the marmalade and sandwich together with the other slice of bread.

3. Place the sandwich in the egg mixture and leave to stand for a few minutes to soak some of it up. Turn the sandwich over and leave to stand until all the egg mixture is absorbed.

4. Preheat the air fryer to 200°C (400°F). Spritz the sandwich with a little oil and cook for 4 minutes. Turn it over, spritz with a little more oil and cook for a further 3–4 minutes until golden.

5. Allow to cool slightly then cut in half to serve.

KING OYSTER MUSHROOM BREAKFAST SANDWICH

Serves: 1
Ready in: 12 minutes, plus 10 minutes marinating time

For the mushroom filling:
1 tbsp dark soy sauce
1 tsp smoked paprika
2 tsp maple syrup
½ tsp sunflower oil
salt and freshly ground black pepper
1 large king oyster mushroom, cut
    into thin slices

2 slices vegan seeded bread
1 tsp vegan spread
1 tomato, sliced
½ ripe avocado, peeled, stoned
    and sliced

1. In a shallow dish, mix together the soy sauce, smoked paprika, maple syrup, oil and seasoning. Stir well. Add the mushrooms, turn them in the sauce and then leave to marinate for 10 minutes at room temperature.

2. Preheat the air fryer to 200°C (400°F). Place the mushrooms in a single layer in the air fryer and cook for 8–10 minutes, turning once and brushing with any remaining marinade until they start to crisp.

3. Meanwhile, spread one slice of the bread with the vegan spread, then add the tomato and avocado slices. When the mushrooms are cooked, place them on top and cover with the other slice of bread. Cut the sandwich in half and serve immediately.

LUNCH & LIGHT BITES

ROASTED RED PEPPER AND TOMATO SOUP

Serves: 1
Ready in: 20 minutes

200g (7 oz) vine-ripened tomatoes, halved
1 red pepper, cored, deseeded and cut into 2.5cm (1 inch) pieces
1 small onion, cut into 6 wedges
2 fat cloves of garlic, in their skin
2 sprigs of fresh thyme
salt and freshly ground black pepper
2 tsp olive oil
100ml (⅓ cup) hot vegetable stock or boiling water

To serve:
1 tsp vegan basil pesto
crusty bread

1. Place the tomatoes, peppers, onion, garlic, thyme and seasoning in a bowl. Drizzle over the oil and stir well.

2. Preheat the air fryer to 180°C (350°F). Add the vegetables to the air fryer and cook for 15 minutes, shaking halfway through until softened.

3. Squeeze the cooked garlic out of its skin into a food processor, or a jug if hand blending. Remove the thyme stems and add the leaves to the garlic along with the tomatoes, peppers and onions. Add the stock or water and blend until the soup is smooth but still retains a bit of texture.

4. Transfer to a soup bowl, top with a little pesto and serve with crusty bread.

TUNA AND AVOCADO QUESADILLA

Serves: 1
Ready in: 10 minutes

½ ripe avocado, peeled and stoned
2 tsp lime juice
80g (3 oz) canned tuna in brine,
  drained
2 tbsp canned sweetcorn, drained
2 tbsp tomato salsa (from a jar or
  fresh), plus extra for serving
1 regular flour tortilla
25g (¼ cup) mozzarella cheese,
  grated
sunflower oil, for spritzing

To serve:
mixed salad, extra tomato salsa

1. In a small bowl, mash the avocado with the lime juice. In another bowl, mix the tuna with the sweetcorn and salsa.

2. Lay the tortilla on a board and spread the mashed avocado over one half. Spoon the tuna mixture on top of the avocado and then sprinkle with the mozzarella cheese. Fold the tortilla over the top of the filling and press down. Spritz with a little oil.

3. Preheat the air fryer to 180°C (350°F). Add the tortilla and cook for 4 minutes, then carefully turn it over, spritz with a little more oil and cook for a further 3–4 minutes until the tortilla is toasted and the cheese has melted.

4. Cut into 2 wedges and serve with mixed salad and extra salsa.

RED PEPPER HUMMUS WITH PITTA CHIPS

Serves: 1, with 1–2 extra portions of hummus
Ready in: about 20 minutes

1 red pepper, cored, deseeded and
 cut into quarters
120g (¾ cup) canned chickpeas,
 drained and rinsed
1 small clove of garlic, peeled
1 tbsp tahini (sesame-seed paste)
2 tsp lemon juice
1 tbsp extra virgin olive oil
salt and freshly ground black pepper
paprika, for sprinkling

For the pitta chips:
1 Greek-style flatbread
½ tsp olive oil
1 tsp za'atar (Middle Eastern herb
 mix)
salt and freshly ground black pepper

To serve:
vegetable crudités, such as carrots
 and cucumber

1. Preheat the air fryer to 200°C (400°F). Place the peppers skin-side up inside and cook for 8–10 minutes until the skin is blackened. Place in a food bag and allow to cool slightly.

2. When the peppers are cool enough to handle, remove the blackened skins. Place the skinned peppers on paper towels to remove any excess moisture.

3. Rub the chickpeas with paper towels to remove any loose skins, then place in in a food processor, reserving a few for serving. Add the peppers and remaining ingredients, blend until smooth and creamy and then season to taste.

4. For the pitta chips, preheat the air fryer to 180°C (350°F). Cut the flatbread into 8 triangles. Place in a bowl, drizzle over the oil and season with the za'atar and a little salt and black pepper. Toss until evenly coated, then cook in a single layer for 4 minutes, turning once, until crisp.

5. Serve the hummus in a bowl, sprinkled with a little paprika and the reserved chickpeas, with the pitta chips and crudités for dipping. Store any leftover hummus in an airtight container in the fridge for 3–4 days.

ROASTED VEGETABLE AND HUMMUS CIABATTA ROLL

Serves: 1, with leftover roasted vegetables
Ready in: about 20 minutes

½ small red pepper and ½ small
  yellow pepper, cut into chunks
½ courgette (zucchini), thickly sliced
½ small red onion, cut into 4 wedges
1 tsp olive oil
1 clove of garlic, crushed
½ tsp dried mixed herbs
salt and freshly ground black pepper
4 cherry tomatoes
1 tsp balsamic vinegar
2 tbsp hummus, or roasted red
  pepper hummus (see page 37)
1 ciabatta roll, halved
a handful of rocket (arugula) leaves

1. Preheat the air fryer to 180°C (350°F). Place all the vegetables except for the tomatoes in a bowl, add the oil, garlic and dried herbs, season well, then toss to coat. Cook in the air fryer for 8 minutes, shaking the basket once during cooking.

2. Add the tomatoes and cook for a further 3–4 minutes until they start to burst and the vegetables are tender and roasted. Transfer to a bowl, squash the tomatoes with the back of a fork and drizzle the roasted vegetables with the balsamic vinegar. Stir well and allow to cool slightly.

3. Cut the ciabatta roll in half, spread the base with the hummus then top with a generous amount of the roasted vegetables and a handful of rocket (arugula) leaves.

4. Cut in half and serve immediately.

Tip: Any remaining roasted vegetables can be stored in an airtight container in the fridge for up to 3 days. They are delicious stirred into pasta.

FRITTATA WITH COURGETTE, PEAS, RICOTTA AND MINT

Serves: 1
Ready in: about 18 minutes

½ small courgette (zucchini), grated
25g (¼ cup) frozen peas
1 medium egg
2 tbsp ricotta cheese
salt and freshly ground black pepper
6 mint leaves, chopped
pinch of dried chilli flakes
¼ tsp sunflower oil

To serve:
rocket (arugula) leaves
cherry tomatoes

1. Place the grated courgette (zucchini) in a clean tea towel (kitchen towel) and squeeze out the excess water. Place the peas in a small bowl and cover with cold water, leave to defrost, then drain well.

2. In a jug, whisk together the egg and ricotta cheese and season well. Stir in the courgette, peas, mint and chilli flakes.

3. Preheat the air fryer to 180°C (350°F). Add the oil to the bottom of a 10cm (4 inch) non-stick metal tin and heat in the air fryer for 2 minutes. Swirl the oil around to coat the sides of the tin.

4. Pour the egg mixture into the tin and cook for 9–10 minutes until golden on top and cooked through.

5. Leave to stand in the tin for 2 minutes, then gently remove and serve with rocket (arugula) leaves and a few cherry tomatoes.

CHICKPEA AND CAULIFLOWER BUDDHA BOWL

Serves: 1
Ready in: 20 minutes

120g (¾ cup) canned chickpeas,
   drained and rinsed
6 small cauliflower florets
1 clove of garlic, crushed
½ tsp ground cumin
½ tsp ground coriander
½ tsp smoked paprika
½ tsp salt and freshly ground black
   pepper
2 tsp olive oil
50g (¼ cup) cooked quinoa or mixed
   grains, from a pouch
¼ cucumber, halved lengthways and
   thinly sliced
4 cherry tomatoes, halved

For the tahini dressing:
1 tbsp tahini (sesame-seed paste)
1 tbsp cold water
1 tsp lemon juice

To serve:
1 lemon wedge

1. Place the chickpeas, cauliflower, garlic, spices and oil in a bowl. Season with the dried spices and toss well to coat.

2. Preheat the air fryer to 180°C (350°F). Add the chickpeas and cauliflower to the air fryer and cook for 12 minutes, shaking halfway through.

3. Meanwhile, in a small bowl mix together the dressing ingredients and season to taste.

4. Place the quinoa or mixed grains, cucumber and tomatoes in sections in a bowl. Top with the cauliflower and crispy chickpeas and drizzle over the tahini dressing. Serve with the lemon wedge to squeeze over.

FLATBREAD PIZZA

Serves: 1
Ready in: 9–10 minutes

1 piadina flatbread or flour tortilla,
about 20cm (8 inch)

For the Greek one:
1 tbsp sundried-tomato pesto
50g (⅓ cup) feta cheese, crumbled
into pieces
a few slices of red onion
a few slices of pitted black olive
4 cherry tomatoes, halved
a pinch of dried mixed herbs

For the Italian one:
1 tbsp basil pesto, plus a little extra
for drizzling
2 slices of Parma ham
120g (4½ oz) mozzarella cheese,
drained well and torn into
small pieces
1 tomato, sliced
4 chargrilled antipasti artichokes
1 tbsp Parmesan cheese, freshly grated

For the American vegan one:
1 tbsp barbeque sauce
50g (2 oz) canned jackfruit, drained,
shredded and mixed with another
1 tbsp barbeque sauce
6 pieces of canned pineapple
6 slices of red pepper
6 jalapeños from a jar, drained
2 tbsp vegan mozzarella, grated

1. Preheat the air fryer to 180°C (350°F). Place the flatbread inside the basket and cook for 2 minutes until starting to crisp.

2. Remove the basket and turn the bread over. Spoon over the sauce and add the other toppings.

3. Return the basket to the air fryer and cook for 4–5 minutes until the pizza is crispy and the topping melted.

4. Serve immediately garnished with some basil leaves if desired and a handful of salad leaves.

Tip: The beauty of this pizza is that you can create your own with your favourite toppings or whatever you have in the fridge. If the flatbread doesn't fit in your air fryer cut it into 4 triangles.

CHICKEN CAESAR SALAD

Serves: 1
Ready in: about 20 minutes

1 × 150g (5 oz) boneless, skinless
   chicken breast
½ tsp freshly ground black pepper
olive oil, for spritzing
½ heart Romaine lettuce, trimmed
   and leaves torn
½ avocado, peeled, stoned and
   thinly sliced
a few Parmesan cheese shavings

For the croutons:
1 thick slice of ciabatta, cut into
   2.5cm (1 inch) cubes
1 tsp olive oil
1 tsp Parmesan cheese, freshly grated
salt and freshly ground black pepper

For the Caesar dressing:
2 tbsp fat-free Greek yogurt
1 tsp lemon juice
1 tbsp Parmesan cheese, freshly
   grated
1 small clove of garlic, crushed
½ tsp Dijon mustard
1 tsp extra virgin olive oil
¼ tsp anchovy paste or
   Worcestershire sauce

1. Preheat the air fryer to 180°C (350°F).
   Season the chicken on both sides with
   the black pepper then spritz with a little
   oil. Cook in the air fryer for 12–15 minutes,
   turning halfway through and spritzing with
   a little more oil until cooked through.

2. Meanwhile, place the ciabatta cubes in a
   bowl, add the oil, Parmesan and seasoning
   and toss to coat. Add to the air fryer with
   the chicken for the last 4–5 minutes of
   cooking time, shaking the basket once,
   until golden brown and crisp. Remove
   everything from the air fryer and leave
   to cool.

3. While the chicken and croutons are
   cooking, make the dressing. Place all the
   ingredients in a small bowl and stir until
   well combined.

4. Place the lettuce in a bowl and stir in
   half the dressing to coat the leaves. Slice
   the chicken, add to the lettuce with the
   avocado and scatter over the croutons.

5. Drizzle over the remaining dressing and
   add some Parmesan cheese shavings.
   Serve immediately.

CRISPY SESAME TOFU WITH MISO DRESSING

Serves: 1

Ready in: 15 minutes, plus 10 minutes marinating

1 tsp dark soy sauce

1 tsp rice wine vinegar

125g (4½ oz) firm tofu, cut into 1.5cm (¾ inch) slices

1 tbsp mixed black and white sesame seeds

sunflower oil, for spritzing

125g (4½ oz) mangetout (snow peas), thinly sliced

1 small carrot, peeled and sliced into ribbons with a vegetable peeler

1 spring onion (green onion), thinly sliced

50g (¼ cup) cooked edamame beans

125g (¾ cup) cooked black and white quinoa, from a pouch

For the miso dressing:

2 tsp white miso paste

½ tsp maple syrup

½ tsp ginger paste

juice of ½ a lime

1. Mix together the soy sauce and vinegar in a bowl and stir to mix, then add the tofu slices, turn to coat and leave to marinate for about 10 minutes.

2. Meanwhile, whisk together all the dressing ingredients in a small bowl. Set aside.

3. Place the sesame seeds on a flat plate, then remove the tofu slices from the marinade and press them into the seeds to coat them all over.

4. Preheat the air fryer to 180°C (350°F). Spritz the tofu slices with a little oil and cook in the air fryer for 10 minutes, turning halfway through and spritzing with a little more oil until golden and crispy.

5. Heat the quinoa according to pack instructions and transfer to a clean bowl. Stir in the mangetout (snow peas), carrots, spring onion (green onion) and edamame beans and most of the dressing.

6. Place the tofu over the top, drizzle with the remaining dressing and serve immediately.

HALLOUMI TOASTIE WITH HONEY HARISSA

Serves: 1

Ready in: about 12 minutes

2 tsp honey

1 tsp harissa paste

2 medium slices of bread, such as
sourdough or bloomer

1 tomato, sliced

50g (2 oz) halloumi cheese or Cypriot
grilling cheese, grated

2 tsp butter, melted for spreading

1. Mix together the honey and harissa in a small bowl. Spread each slice of the bread with the mixture.

2. Arrange the slices of tomato on top of the harissa on one slice of bread and sprinkle over the cheese.

3. Top with the other slice of bread, harissa-side down, then spread the top with some of the butter.

4. Preheat the air fryer to 190°C (375°F). Place the toastie inside, butter-side down, then brush the top with the remaining butter. Cook for 4 minutes, then carefully flip over and cook for a further 3–4 minutes until the cheese has melted and the bread is toasted.

5. Cut in half and serve immediately.

ASIAN-STYLE TUNA, MANGO AND AVOCADO SALAD

Serves: 1
Ready in: 15 minutes

½ ripe mango, peeled, stoned and chopped
½ ripe avocado, peeled, stoned and sliced
3 radishes, thinly sliced
3cm (1¼ inch) piece of cucumber, halved, seeds removed and thinly sliced
1 tbsp fresh coriander (cilantro), roughly chopped
1 × 120–125g (4–4½ oz) tuna steak, about 1cm (¼ inch) thick
sesame oil, for brushing
freshly ground black pepper
50g (2½ cups) mixed salad leaves

For the dressing:
finely grated zest and juice of ½ a lime
2 tsp Thai sweet chilli sauce
1 tsp light soy sauce
1 tsp freshly grated ginger

1. Place the mango pieces and avocado slices in a bowl with any juice from the mango, then add the cucumber, radishes and coriander (cilantro).

2. Preheat the air fryer to 180°C (350°F). Brush the tuna steak on both sides with a little sesame oil, then season with black pepper and cook in the air fryer for 6 minutes, turning halfway through, for a medium steak. Remove and thinly slice.

3. Mix together all the dressing ingredients. Pour half the dressing over the salad in the bowl and gently toss together.

4. Arrange the salad leaves on a plate or in a shallow bowl and top with the mango and avocado mixture. Place the sliced tuna over the top and drizzle over the remaining dressing. Serve immediately.

SPEEDY SUPPERS

BAKED FETA AND SQUASH PASTA

Serves: 1
Ready in: 20 minutes

125g (4 oz) peeled butternut squash,
  cut into 1.5cm (¾ inch) pieces
1 tsp olive oil
Pinch of chilli flakes
salt and freshly ground black pepper
4 sage leaves
50g (2 oz) block feta cheese
100g (4 oz) dried rigatoni or penne
  pasta
25g (1¼ cup) baby spinach

1. Place the squash in an ovenproof dish that fits your air fryer. Drizzle over the olive oil, sprinkle over the chilli flakes and season with freshly ground black pepper.

2. Preheat the air fryer to 190°C (375°F). Cook the squash for 5 minutes. Nestle the feta in the middle. Cook for a further 10 minutes, stirring the squash once, and adding the sage leaves, until the squash is tender and the feta has softened.

3. Meanwhile cook the pasta in a pan of boiling water, for about 10 minutes or according to pack instructions until just tender. Stir in the spinach to wilt and drain, reserving 2 tablespoons of the cooking water.

4. Stir the drained pasta and spinach into the squash and feta with 1–2 tablespoons of the reserved water to make a creamy sauce.

5. Place in a bowl and serve immediately with freshly ground black pepper.

VIETNAMESE SEABASS

Serves: 1

Ready in: about 18 minutes

1 pak choi (bok choy), end trimmed,
   stem sliced and leaves separated
1 small carrot, peeled and thinly
   sliced
75g (3 oz) shitake mushrooms, sliced
2cm (¾ inch) piece of fresh ginger,
   peeled and cut into thin strips
1 spring onion (green onion), thinly
   sliced
1 tsp toasted sesame oil
1 seabass fillet, skin scored 3 times
freshly ground black pepper

For the sauce:
1 tbsp oyster sauce
1 tbsp dark soy sauce
1 tsp Thai fish sauce
juice of a ½ lime
a pinch of chilli flakes

To serve:
1 × 50g (2 oz) nest of flat rice noodles
6 fresh mint leaves

1. Place the pak choi (bok choy) stems in a bowl with the carrot, mushrooms, ginger and spring onion (green onion) and drizzle over the oil.

2. Preheat the air fryer to 190°C (375°F). Place the vegetables in the air fryer and cook for 5 minutes.

3. Meanwhile, mix together all the sauce ingredients in a bowl.

4. Season the fish with a little black pepper. Place skin-side up in the air fryer with the vegetables and cook for 4 minutes.

5. Remove the fish to a plate, tip the vegetables into the base of air fryer, removing the rack, and add the pak choi leaves. Pour over ¾ of the sauce, stir to coat the vegetables, then return the fish flesh-side up. Spoon the remaining sauce over the fish and cook for 2–3 minutes.

6. While the sea bass is cooking, prepare the noodles according to pack instructions.

7. Serve the noodles on a plate, topped with the vegetables and seabass, drizzling over any sauce. Scatter over the mint leaves and serve immediately.

PARMESAN AND BASIL CHICKEN SCHNITZEL WITH GARLIC AND HERB POTATOES

Serves: 1
Ready in: 24 minutes

1 × 150g (5 oz) skinless, boneless
   chicken breast
1 tbsp plain flour
salt and freshly ground black pepper
1 egg, beaten
2 tbsp panko breadcrumbs
2 tbsp Parmesan cheese, freshly
   grated
1 tbsp fresh basil, chopped
1 medium potato, peeled and cut
   into 1.5cm cubes (¾ inch)
1 tsp olive oil, plus extra for spritzing
1 clove of garlic, crushed
½ tsp dried mixed herbs
6 cherry tomatoes, on the vine

To serve:
rocket (arugula) leaves
1 lemon wedge

1. Place the chicken breast between 2 sheets of baking (parchment) paper and flatten with a rolling pin to 5mm (¼ inch) thick.

2. Place the flour on a plate and season. Mix together the breadcrumbs, Parmesan cheese and basil in another bowl.

3. Coat the chicken in the flour, shaking off any excess, then dip in the egg and finally in the breadcrumbs to fully coat.

4. Toss the potatoes in the oil, garlic and herbs and a little seasoning and toss to coat.

5. Preheat the air fryer to 190°C (375°F). Spritz one side of the chicken with oil and place oil-side down in the air fryer. Arrange the potatoes around the chicken and spritz the top of the chicken with a little more oil. Cook for 12–14 minutes, turning halfway.

6. Add the tomatoes for the last 4 minutes of cooking time until they start to burst, the potatoes are crispy and the chicken golden and cooked through.

7. Transfer to a plate and serve immediately with some rocket leaves and the wedge of lemon to squeeze over the chicken.

BAKED SALMON WITH NEW POTATOES, ASPARAGUS AND LEMON AND DILL SAUCE

Serves: 1
Ready in: 20 minutes

4 baby new potatoes, halved
6–7 asparagus spears, woody ends
  snapped off
½ tsp olive oil, plus extra for
  spritzing
salt and freshly ground black pepper
1 × 150–175g (5–6 oz) salmon fillet,
  skin on

For the lemon and dill sauce:
2 tbsp crème fraîche
2 tsp lemon juice
1 tbsp fresh dill, chopped
1 tsp finely grated lemon zest

1. Place the new potatoes and asparagus in a bowl, drizzle over the oil and season.

2. Preheat the air fryer to 180°C (350°F). Add the potatoes and cook for 5 minutes.

3. Add the salmon fillet to the air fryer, skin-side down, and season with black pepper. Cook for 9–10 minutes, adding the asparagus and turning the potatoes halfway through.

4. While the salmon is cooking, mix together the sauce ingredients in a small bowl. Check the salmon is cooked through and flakes easily and the potatoes and asparagus are tender.

5. Transfer to a plate, top the salmon with the sauce and serve immediately.

ROASTED SPICY CAULIFLOWER STEAK WITH BLACK BEAN AND CORN SALAD

Serves: 1

Ready in: about 20 minutes

1 tbsp siracha sauce
1 tbsp maple syrup
1 lime
1 large or 2 small cauliflower steaks, about 3cm (1 inch) thick
¼ tsp ground cumin
½ tsp olive oil

For the salad:

100g (½ cup) canned black beans, drained, rinsed
4 cherry tomatoes, quartered
50g (½ cup) red cabbage, shredded
2 tbsp canned sweetcorn, drained
1 tbsp fresh coriander (cilantro), chopped
a pinch of salt

To serve:

½ ripe avocado or 1 ripe baby avocado, peeled, stoned and sliced
1 tbsp plant-based natural yogurt
a pinch of smoked paprika

1. In a medium bowl, mix together the siracha sauce, maple syrup, cumin and olive oil. Finely grate in the zest from the lime, then squeeze in the juice of half the lime, reserving the other half. Stir well, add the cauliflower steak and turn to coat.

2. Preheat the air fryer to 180°C (350°F). Place the cauliflower steak in the air fryer, brush with the sauce and cook for 12–15 minutes, turning halfway through and brushing with more sauce, until tender and lightly charred.

3. Meanwhile, place all the salad ingredients in a bowl and squeeze over the juice of the reserved half lime. Stir well and leave to stand while the cauliflower steak is cooking.

4. Pile the salad onto a plate, top with the cauliflower and drizzle with any remaining sauce from the bowl. Top with slices of avocado and the yogurt sprinkled with a little paprika. Serve immediately.

SPEEDY SUPPERS

PANCETTA-WRAPPED COD WITH CREAMY LEMON BUTTER BEANS

Serves: 1
Ready in: about 18 minutes

120g (¾ cup) canned butter beans (lima beans), drained and rinsed
100ml (⅓ cup) hot vegetable stock
1 sprig of fresh rosemary
1 clove of garlic, crushed
1 tbsp crème fraîche
zest of 1 small lemon, finely grated
1 tbsp lemon juice
1 × 150g (5 oz) cod loin
salt and freshly ground black pepper
1 slice of pancetta
6 tenderstem broccoli (broccolini) tips

1. Preheat the air fryer to 180°C (350°F). Place the butter beans (lima beans), stock, rosemary sprig, garlic, crème fraîche and half the lemon zest in an ovenproof dish and stir well. Cook in the air fryer for 10 minutes, stirring halfway through until bubbling. Stir in the lemon juice.

2. Meanwhile, coat the cod with the remaining lemon zest and season with a little black pepper, then wrap with the slice of pancetta.

3. Place the tenderstem broccoli (broccolini) over the beans and nestle the cod on top. Cook for a further 8 minutes until the pancetta is crispy, the tenderstem broccoli tender, and the cod cooked through and flakes easily.

4. Remove the rosemary sprig and place the creamy beans in a shallow bowl. Top with the cod and broccoli, season and serve immediately.

HARISSA-SPICED AUBERGINES WITH CRISPY CHICKPEAS

Serves: 1
Ready in: 18–20 minutes

½ aubergine (eggplant), cut into 2cm
  (¾ inch) cubes
1 small red onion, cut into 8 wedges
1 clove of garlic, crushed
120g (¾ cup) canned chickpeas,
  drained
1 tsp olive oil
1–2 tsp harissa paste, depending on
  how spicy you like it
2 tsp maple syrup
finely grated zest and juice ½ lemon
salt and freshly ground black pepper
1 tomato, quartered
50g (⅓ cup) dried couscous
1 tbsp fresh flat leaf parsley, chopped
a pinch of dukkah (Egyptian spice
  blend)
1 tbsp pomegranate seeds

To serve:
1 tbsp plant-based Greek-style
  yogurt
1 lemon wedge

1. Place the aubergine (eggplant) cubes, onions, garlic and chickpeas in a bowl and drizzle over the oil. Add the harissa paste, maple syrup, lemon zest and juice and stir to coat evenly. Season well.

2. Preheat the air fryer to 180°C (350°F). Place the vegetables in the air fryer and cook for 12 minutes, shaking halfway through. Add the tomatoes and cook for a further 4 minutes until the aubergine is lightly charred, the chickpeas crispy and the tomatoes softened.

3. Meanwhile, place the couscous in a small bowl and pour over enough boiling water to cover, then cover and leave to stand for about 8 minutes. When all the water has been absorbed, fluff with a fork.

4. Transfer the couscous to a plate, then top with the aubergine and chickpea mixture. Sprinkle over the parsley, pomegranate seeds and dukka and put a spoonful of yogurt on one side. Serve with the lemon wedge to squeeze over.

CHICKEN, GINGER AND CASHEW NUT STIR-FRY

Serves: 1
Ready in: 18 minutes

1 tsp toasted sesame oil
2 tsp freshly grated ginger
1 small clove of garlic, crushed
150g (5 oz) boneless, skinless chicken breast or thighs, thinly sliced
1 small carrot, peeled and cut into thin strips
4 baby corn, halved lengthways
6 mangetout (snow peas), halved if large
2 tbsp cashew nuts
1 × 60g (2 oz) nest of dried medium egg noodles

Sauce:
2 tbsp black-bean sauce
2 tsp soy sauce
2 tsp rice wine vinegar

1. In a medium-sized bowl, mix together the sesame oil, ginger and garlic, then add the chicken slices, carrot and baby corn and stir to coat.

2. Preheat the air fryer to 180°C (350°F). Place the chicken and vegetables in a single layer in the air fryer and cook for 4 minutes. Shake the basket, add the cashew nuts, and cook for a further 2 minutes.

3. Meanwhile, cook the noodles for 3–4 minutes in a pan of boiling water, or according to pack instructions, and drain well. Mix together all the sauce ingredients in a small bowl.

4. Remove the rack and tip the chicken and vegetables into the bottom of the air fryer, adding the noodles, mangetout (snow peas) and sauce. Stir well to coat in the sauce and cook for 2–3 minutes until heated through.

5. Transfer to a bowl and serve immediately.

CRISPY GNOCCHI WITH ROASTED VEGETABLES

Serves: 1

Ready in: about 15 minutes

150g (5 oz) vegan gnocchi

3 tsp olive oil, divided

1 clove of garlic, crushed

¼ tsp chilli flakes

½ tsp smoked paprika

salt and freshly ground black pepper

½ yellow pepper, cut into small
  chunks

8 cherry tomatoes

15g (¾ cup) fresh basil

2 tsp toasted pine nuts

1 tbsp black olives, sliced (optional)

To serve:

crisp green salad

1. Toss the gnocchi in a bowl with the 1 tsp of olive oil, garlic, chilli flakes and smoked paprika. Season well.

2. Preheat the air fryer to 200°C (400°F). Put the gnocchi in the air fryer and cook for 5–6 minutes. Shake the basket, add the pepper and tomatoes and cook for a further 5–6 minutes until the gnocchi is crispy and the tomatoes have burst.

3. While the gnocchi are cooking, place the basil, pine nuts and remaining oil in a small food processor and blitz until finely chopped. Season well.

4. Transfer the gnocchi to a serving bowl, add the olives, if using, and drizzle over the pesto.

5. Serve immediately with a crisp green salad.

CAJUN CHICKEN TRAYBAKE

Serves: 1

Ready in: about 25 minutes

150g (5 oz) boneless, skinless chicken
   thighs

1 × 100g (4 oz) baking potato, washed
   and cut into 4–5 wedges

1 tsp sunflower oil

1 tsp Cajun seasoning

½ small red onion, cut into 4 wedges

½ red pepper and ½ yellow pepper,
   cut into chunks

For the chive yogurt:

1 tbsp fat-free Greek yogurt

2 tsp chives, chopped

juice ¼ lime

To serve:

1 tbsp tomato salsa

1 lime wedge

1. Place the chicken thighs and potato wedges in a bowl, drizzle over the oil, then sprinkle over the spice mix. Stir well, then add the onion and peppers and stir again.

2. Preheat the air fryer to 180°C (350°F). Place the chicken and potato wedges in a single layer in the air fryer and cook for 10 minutes. Turn them over, then gently shake the basket. Cook for a further 10 minutes until cooked through.

3. Meanwhile, in a small bowl, mix together the yogurt, chives and the lime juice.

4. Transfer the chicken and vegetables to a plate and serve immediately, with the chive yogurt, tomato salsa and the lime wedge, for squeezing over.

GARLIC-STUFFED MUSHROOMS WITH RICOTTA AND SUNDRIED TOMATO

Serves: 1
Ready in: 15 minutes

2 large flat or portobello mushrooms
1 tsp garlic-infused olive oil
salt and freshly ground black pepper

For the filling:
6 large basil leaves, roughly chopped
100g (½ cup) ricotta cheese
2 tsp sundried-tomato pesto
2 tbsp Parmesan cheese, freshly
   grated
2 tbsp toasted pine nuts
1 tbsp dried breadcrumbs

To serve:
rocket (arugula) and tomato salad

1. Remove the mushroom stalks and discard. Brush the mushrooms all over with the garlic oil, then season.

2. Preheat the air fryer to 190°C (375°F). Place the mushrooms into the air fryer skin-side up and cook for 6 minutes.

3. Meanwhile, make the filling. Place the basil in a bowl with the ricotta cheese, pesto and 1 tablespoon of the Parmesan cheese. Stir well to mix, then season.

4. In a small bowl, mix the remaining Parmesan cheese with the breadcrumbs and stir through the pine nuts.

5. Turn the mushrooms over and fill their cavities with the cheese mixture, then top with the breadcrumb mix, pressing it down gently with the back of a spoon.

6. Cook for a further 5–6 minutes until the topping is golden and the mushrooms are cooked through. Serve immediately with rocket (arugula) and tomato salad.

EVERYDAY FAVOURITES

ROAST CHICKEN DINNER

Serves: 1
Ready in: 35 minutes

1 medium-sized potato, peeled and
    cut into 4 pieces
1 small parsnip, peeled and cut into
    thick batons
1 carrot, peeled and cut into thick
    batons
1 tsp olive oil
2 sprigs of fresh thyme
salt and freshly ground black pepper
1 boneless, skinless chicken breast
2 rashers (slices) of smoked streaky
    bacon or pancetta

To serve:
peas
chicken gravy

1. Cook the potato in a pan of salted boiling water for 5 minutes, then add the parsnip and cook for another minute. Drain well, shake to rough up the edges of the potato, then return to the pan with the carrots. Drizzle over the oil and a sprig of thyme, season and toss to coat in the oil.

2. Season the chicken breast with black pepper, top with the remaining sprig of thyme, then wrap with the bacon or pancetta.

3. Preheat the air fryer to 180°C (350°F). Place the chicken and potatoes in the air fryer and cook for 10 minutes. Turn the potatoes, add the parsnips and carrots and cook for a further 10 minutes.

4. Remove the chicken to a plate and cover with foil to rest. Increase the air-fryer temperature to 200°C (400°F) and cook the vegetables for 4 minutes until crispy.

5. Add the roasted vegetables to the plate with the chicken and serve immediately with peas and gravy.

GARLIC AND HERB LAMB CHOPS WITH CRISPY VEGETABLES

Serves: 1
Ready in: about 22 minutes

100g (3½ oz) small new potatoes, halved if large

1 small carrot, peeled and chopped

½ leek, cut into 2.5cm (1 inch) pieces

1 tsp olive oil

salt and freshly ground black pepper

1 clove of garlic, crushed

2 tsp fresh rosemary leaves, finely chopped

2 lamb loin chops, about 100–110g (3.5–4 oz) each

To serve:
gravy

1. Place the potatoes, carrot and leek in a bowl, drizzle over half a teaspoon of the olive oil, season and toss to coat evenly.

2. Place the remaining oil in a shallow dish, add the garlic, rosemary leaves and lamb chops and turn to coat evenly.

3. Preheat the air fryer to 180°C (350°F). Place the vegetables in the air fryer in a single layer and cook for 8 minutes, shaking halfway through.

4. Add the chops to the air fryer and cook for 10–12 minutes, turning halfway through and stirring the vegetables until the chops are cooked through.

5. Transfer the chops and vegetables to a plate and serve immediately with gravy.

SALMON FISHCAKES WITH GARLIC AND HERB FILLING

Makes: 2
Ready in: 20 minutes

1 medium-sized floury potato, peeled
    and chopped
2 tbsp butter
salt and freshly ground black pepper
1 × 105g (3¾ oz) canned skinless and
    boneless pink salmon, drained
1 tbsp flat leaf parsley, chopped
1 tsp finely grated lemon zest
2 tsp light garlic and herb cream
    cheese
1 tbsp plain flour
25g (¼ cup) dried breadcrumbs
1 egg, beaten
sunflower oil, for spritzing

To serve:
broccoli or peas
1 lemon wedge

1. Cook the potatoes in a small pan of lightly salted boiling water for 10 minutes until tender. Drain well, then return to the pan, mash with the butter and season to taste. Transfer to a bowl and leave to cool.

2. Flake the salmon and add to the potatoes with the parsley and lemon zest. Season well and stir gently to mix. Shape into 2 balls. Press your thumb into the middle of the balls to make a well, then fill each with a teaspoon of the garlic and herb cream cheese. Remould the top so the cream cheese is encased, then flatten slightly to form a fishcake.

3. Place the flour and breadcrumbs on separate flat plates and the egg in a bowl. Lightly dust the fishcakes in the flour, then place in the egg and brush the sides and top so they are fully coated. Coat with the breadcrumbs, patting the crumbs on the sides and tops so they are lightly covered.

4. Preheat the air fryer to 180°C (350°F). Place the fishcakes in the air fryer, spritz with a little oil and cook for 13–15 minutes, turning halfway through and spritzing with more oil until golden and crispy.

5. Serve immediately with broccoli or peas and the lemon wedge to squeeze over.

BAKED MUSHROOM RISOTTO

Serves: 1

Ready in: about 27 minutes, plus 15 minutes soaking time

15g (¼ cup) dried porcini mushrooms

125ml (½ cup) boiling water

2 tbsp butter

1 tsp olive oil

½ onion, finely chopped

1 clove of garlic, crushed

4 chestnut (brown button) mushrooms, quartered

75g (generous ⅓ cup) risotto (arborio) rice

300ml (1¼ cup) hot vegetable stock

2 tbsp Parmesan cheese, freshly grated

1 tbsp flat leaf parsley, chopped

salt and freshly ground black pepper

To serve:

rocket (arugula) leaves

Parmesan shavings

1. Place the porcini mushrooms in a small bowl, pour over the boiling water and leave to soak for 15 minutes.

2. Preheat the air fryer to 180°C (350°F). Place the butter and oil in a deep ovenproof dish or cake tin and heat in the air fryer for 1 minute. Stir in the onion and garlic and cook for 2 minutes until softened. Drain the porcini mushrooms, reserving the soaking liquid. Roughly chop, then add them along with the chestnut (brown button) mushrooms to the onions and stir well. Cook for 4 minutes, then stir in the rice and cook for another minute.

3. Pour over the reserved mushroom liquid and cook for 4 minutes. Stir in 150ml (⅔ cup) of the stock and cook for 10 minutes, stirring halfway through.

4. Stir in remaining stock and cook for a further 8–10 minutes, stirring once, until most of the stock has been absorbed and the rice is just tender. Stir in the grated Parmesan cheese and parsley. Season to taste.

5. Transfer to a bowl and serve with the rocket (arugula) leaves and Parmesan cheese shavings.

CREAMY CHICKEN AND LEEK FILO PIE

Serves: 1
Ready in: about 20 minutes

75g (2½ oz) leek, sliced

125g (4½ oz) boneless, skinless
  chicken breast or thigh, cut into
  1.5cm (¾ inch) pieces

1½ tsp sunflower oil

salt and freshly ground black pepper

3 tbsp light cream cheese

1 tsp wholegrain mustard

2 tbsp milk

½ tsp fresh thyme leaves

1 44 × 25cm sheet (17x9½ inches)
  filo pastry

To serve:

carrots and tenderstem broccoli
  (broccolini)

1. Preheat the air fryer to 180°C (350°F). Place the leeks, chicken and half a teaspoon of the oil in a bowl and season with salt and pepper. Place the leeks and chicken in a single layer in the air fryer and cook for 8 minutes, shaking halfway through.

2. Meanwhile, mix together the cream cheese, mustard, milk and thyme in a small bowl. Stir in the chicken and leek mixture.

3. Place the mixture in a 250ml (1 cup) ovenproof dish and cook at 160°C (325°F) for 3–4 minutes, to heat the sauce through. Stir well.

4. Cut the sheet of filo pastry in half, lightly brush one half with some of the remaining oil, then place the other half on top and brush with the rest of the oil. Cut into 4 squares. Scrunch up each square and place on top of the chicken and leek mixture. Cook for a further 8 minutes until the mixture is bubbling and the pastry is golden and crisp.

5. Serve immediately with carrots and tenderstem (broccolini).

CRISPY PANKO FISH AND CHIPS

Serves: 1
Ready in: about 25 minutes

For the fish:
1 × 150g (5 oz) skinless cod or
   haddock fillet
25g (¼ cup) panko breadcrumbs
2 tsp sunflower oil
1 tbsp plain flour
Salt and freshly ground pepper
1 egg, beaten
1 tsp finely grated lemon zest

For the chips:
1 medium-sized Maris Piper or King
   Edward potato, peeled and cut into
   1.5cm (¾ inch) thick chips
1 tsp olive oil
salt

To serve:
mushy or fresh peas
tartare sauce
1 lemon wedge

1. Preheat the air fryer to 180°C (350°F). Put the sunflower oil in a small ovenproof dish and heat for 2 minutes. Add the panko breadcrumbs and stir to coat. Cook for 2–3 minutes, stirring once, until lightly golden. Allow to cool.

2. Toss the chips with the olive oil and salt.

3. Place the flour, beaten egg and panko breadcrumbs in 3 separate bowls. Season the flour with salt and pepper. Add the lemon zest to the panko breadcrumbs and mix well.

4. Dry the fish fillet with a paper towel. Coat in the seasoned flour, then dip in the egg to coat fully, then press into the breadcrumbs to coat.

5. Preheat the air fryer to 180°C (350°F). Place the fish in the middle, then place the chips around the edge. Cook for 12–14 minutes, turning everything halfway through until the fish is golden, crispy and cooked through and the chips are golden.

6. Transfer to a plate and serve immediately with mushy peas or fresh peas, tartare sauce and a wedge of lemon for squeezing over the fish.

SPINACH AND RICOTTA CANNELLONI

Serves: 1
Ready in: about 25–30 minutes

150g (¾ cup) fresh baby spinach
75g (⅓ cup) ricotta cheese
a pinch of ground nutmeg
2 tsp finely grated lemon zest
1 tbsp Parmesan cheese, freshly
    grated
salt and freshly ground black pepper
1 large sheet of fresh lasagne pasta
olive oil, for spritzing
200ml (¾ cup) passata (tomato
    sauce) with onions and garlic
1 tbsp fresh basil, chopped
15g Cheddar cheese, grated

To serve:
rocket (arugula) leaves

1. Place the spinach in a sieve (strainer) and pour over boiling water to wilt. Allow to cool, then squeeze out the excess water.

2. In a small bowl, mix together the ricotta, nutmeg, lemon zest and Parmesan cheese. Season well. Chop the spinach and stir into the ricotta mixture.

3. Cut the lasagne sheet in half. Place in a bowl and cover with water and leave to soften slightly for 2 minutes. Remove and drain well.

4. Lightly spritz an ovenproof dish with the oil. Mix the passata (tomato sauce) with the basil and spoon half into the bottom of the dish. Divide the ricotta mixture between the lasagne sheets, along the bottom edge, then roll the sheets into 2 tubes.

5. Place the tubes in the dish, seam-side down, pour over the remaining passata and sprinkle with the Cheddar cheese.

6. Preheat the air fryer to 180°C (350°F). Place the dish of cannelloni inside and cook for 15–20 minutes until golden and bubbling.

7. Transfer to a plate and serve immediately with rocket (arugula) leaves.

EVERYDAY FAVOURITES

SAUSAGE, VEGETABLE AND PUY-LENTIL BAKE

Serves: 1
Ready in: about 23 minutes

1 small leek, cut into 1cm (¼ inch)
   slices
1 carrot, peeled and cut into 1cm
   (¼ inch) slices
2 pork sausages
½ tsp cumin seeds
1 sprig fresh thyme
1 tsp olive oil
salt and freshly ground black pepper
125g (½ cup) cooked puy lentils
125ml (½ cup) hot chicken stock
50g (1½ oz) cavolo nero (Tuscan kale)
   or kale, shredded

1. Preheat the air fryer to 180°C (350°F). Place the leek, carrot, sausages, cumin seeds and thyme in a bowl, drizzle with the oil and season well. Toss to coat, then place in a single layer in the air fryer and cook for 10 minutes, shaking halfway through.

2. Tip the sausages and vegetables into the base of the air fryer, remove the rack and add the lentils, stock and cavolo nero (Tuscan kale) or kale. Cook for a further 8 minutes, stirring once, until the sausages are cooked through and the vegetables tender.

3. Remove the thyme, transfer to a bowl and serve immediately.

PORK AND APPLE BURGERS WITH SWEET POTATO FRIES

Serves: 1
Ready in: about 20 minutes

For the burgers:
1 small eating apple, cored
salt and freshly ground black pepper
100g (3½ oz) lean minced pork
  (ground pork)
3 tsp Cheddar cheese, finely grated
1 tsp dried mixed herbs
1 tsp Dijon mustard

For the fries:
½ small sweet potato, scrubbed and
  sliced into 5mm-thick (¼ inch) fries
½ tsp sunflower oil, plus extra for
  spritzing

To serve:
salad leaves

1. Cut the apple in half, horizontally, then coarsely grate 1 half and cut the other into 3 rings. Pat the grated apple with a piece of paper towel, then place in a bowl with the remaining burger ingredients. Season well.

2. Mix well until all the ingredients are combined, then shape into a burger.

3. Place the sweet potato fries in a small bowl, then add the oil, season and toss well to coat.

4. Preheat the air fryer to 180°C (350°F). Add the burgers and spritz with a little oil, then arrange the fries in a single layer around the burger. Cook for 14–16 minutes, turning halfway through, until the juices run clear. Remove the burger to a warmed plate.

5. Meanwhile, press the grated cheese onto the apple rings. Increase the air-fryer temperature to 200°C (400°F), add the apple rings to the basket and cook for 3 minutes until the topping is golden and the fries are crispy.

6. Add the cheesy apple rings and sweet potato fries to the plate with the burger and serve immediately with salad.

CANNELLINI AND MUSHROOM BALLS PASTA BAKE

Serves: 1
Ready in: about 25 minutes

For the balls:
100g (3½ oz) chestnut (brown button) mushrooms, roughly chopped
1 clove garlic, crushed
½ small onion, roughly chopped into chunks
1 tsp olive oil, plus extra for spritzing
120g (¾ cup) canned cannellini beans, rinsed and drained well
2 tsp dried breadcrumbs
1 tsp vegan sundried-tomato paste
1 tsp dried mixed herbs
salt and freshly ground black pepper

For the sauce:
½ tsp garlic
200g (¾ cup) canned chopped tomatoes
1 tsp vegan sundried-tomato paste
1 tsp balsamic vinegar
1 tsp dried oregano
½ tsp paprika
salt and freshly ground black pepper

75g (2½ oz) dried penne pasta
2 tsp vegan hard cheese, finely grated

To serve:
fresh basil leaves

1. Preheat the air fryer to 180°C (350°F). Place the mushrooms, garlic and onions in a bowl, add the oil and toss well. Place in the air fryer and cook for 8 minutes, shaking once, until softened. Leave to cool slightly, then place in a food processor and pulse until finely chopped. Add all the remaining ball ingredients, season and pulse until the mixture comes together.

2. Mix together all the sauce ingredients in a bowl and season to taste.

3. Shape the vegetable mixture into 4 balls. Place them in the air fryer and cook for 8 minutes. Remove to a plate.

4. While the balls are cooking, cook the pasta in a pan of slightly salted boiling water for 10–12 minutes until tender or according to packet instructions. Drain well. Return to the warm pan and stir in the tomato sauce. Transfer to an ovenproof dish, nestle in the cooked balls and sprinkle with the cheese.

5. Place the dish in the air fryer and cook for 5–6 minutes until the topping is golden and the sauce is bubbling.

6. Transfer to a plate and garnish with fresh basil leaves to serve.

JACKFRUIT AND SWEET POTATO CHILLI

Serves: 1
Ready in: 20 minutes

50g (2 oz) sweet potato, peeled and
   cut into small cubes
½ red onion, chopped
200g (1 cup) canned jackfruit, drained
½ red pepper, cut into cubes
1 tsp ground cumin
1 tsp sunflower oil
1 × 227g (8 oz) canned chopped
   tomatoes
2 tsp chipotle paste (adobo sauce)
60g (¼ cup) canned kidney beans,
   drained and rinsed
100ml (⅓ cup) boiling water
salt and freshly ground black pepper
1 tbsp coriander (cilantro), chopped

To serve:
rice (optional)
plant-based natural yogurt
1 lime wedge

1. Place the sweet potato, onion, jackfruit, red pepper and cumin in a bowl, add the oil and stir to coat.

2. Preheat the air fryer to 180°C (350°F). Place the vegetable mix in a single layer in the air fryer and cook for 15 minutes, shaking halfway through.

3. Tip the vegetables into the bottom of the air fryer, remove the rack, and stir in the tomatoes, chipotle paste (adobo sauce), kidney beans and water. Stir well and cook for a further 4–5 minutes until the vegetables are tender. Season to taste and stir in the coriander (cilantro).

4. Transfer to a plate and serve with rice, if desired, a spoonful of yogurt and the lime wedge to squeeze over.

FAKEAWAYS

TANDOORI CHICKEN KEBABS WITH CHAPATI, MINT RAITA AND SALAD

Serves: 1

Ready in: 20 minutes, plus 1 hour marinating time

1 boneless, skinless chicken breast, cut into 2.5cm (1 inch) pieces
sunflower oil, for spritzing
½ lemon
1 chapati, naan or roti

For the marinade:
50g (¼ cup) fat-free Greek yogurt
2 tsp freshly grated ginger
1 clove of garlic, crushed
1 tsp garam masala
1 tbsp tandoori masala spice mix
1 tbsp lemon juice
½ tsp salt

For the mint raita:
2.5cm (1 inch) piece of cucumber
pinch of salt
4 tbsp fat-free Greek yogurt
a few cumin seeds
1 tbsp fresh mint, chopped

For the salad:
a few thin slices of red onion
½ tomato, chopped

1. Mix together all the marinade ingredients in a bowl and stir in the chicken. Cover and leave to marinate in the fridge for 1 hour.

2. Make the raita. Cut the cucumber in 2 lengthwise and use a spoon to remove the seeds. Coarsely grate the cucumber and place in a sieve (strainer) set over a bowl, stir in the salt and leave for 15 minutes. Squeeze any excess moisture out of the cucumber and pat dry on paper towels.

3. Place in a bowl with the remaining raita ingredients and stir in.

4. Preheat the air fryer to 180°C (350°F). Thread the chicken onto a small metal or pre-soaked wooden skewer. Place in the air fryer, spritz with a little oil and cook for 10–12 minutes, turning once, until the chicken is cooked through. Add the lemon, cut-side down, and cook for the last 4 minutes until lightly charred and juicy.

5. Warm the bread and put on a plate, then top with some of the raita, the red onion and the tomatoes. Add the chicken, the remaining raita and the lemon for squeezing over. Sprinkle over the remaining mint leaves and serve immediately.

CRISPY CHILLI PORK WITH NOODLES

||||||||||||||||||||||||||||||||||||||||||||||||||||||||||||||||||||||||||||||||||||||||||||||||||||||||||||||||||||||||||||||||||||||||||||||||||||||||||||||||||||||||||||||||

Serves: 1

Ready in: about 15 minutes

150g (5 oz) thin-cut pork steak or
  escalope (cutlets), thinly sliced into
  even strips
1 tbsp cornflour (cornstarch)
½ red pepper, cut into thin strips
1.5cm (¾ inch) piece of fresh ginger,
  peeled and cut into matchsticks
6 slices of red chilli
3 spring onions (green onions), thinly
  sliced
1 tsp sesame oil
sunflower oil, for spritzing
1 × 60g (2 oz) nest of egg noodles

For the marinade:
1 tsp dark soy sauce
½ tsp sesame oil
½ tsp Chinese 5-spice powder
1 clove of garlic, crushed

For the sauce:
2 tbsp rice wine vinegar
2 tbsp dark soy sauce
1 tbsp Thai sweet chilli sauce
1 tbsp tomato ketchup

To serve:
sesame seeds

1. Mix together the marinade ingredients in a small bowl, add the pork and stir to coat. Leave to one side.

2. In another bowl, place the red pepper, ginger, chilli and most of the spring onions, reserving a few for serving. Drizzle over the sesame oil evenly.

3. Mix together the sauce ingredients in a third bowl. On a flat plate, put the pork strips in the cornflour and turn to coat evenly.

4. Preheat the air fryer to 200°C (400°F). Place the pork strips in a single layer in the air fryer, spritz with sunflower oil and cook for 6 minutes. Turn and cook for a further 4–5 minutes until crispy. Transfer to a plate.

5. Place the vegetables in an ovenproof dish and cook for 4 minutes. Stir well, add the sauce and cook for another 2–3 minutes until starting to bubble. Stir in the pork and cook for a further 2 minutes until sticky.

6. Cook the noodles in boiling water for 4 minutes until just tender. Drain well and put in a bowl.

7. Add the crispy pork, vegetables, and sauce, then sprinkle with sesame seeds and garnish with spring onions.

TERIYAKI SALMON

Serves: 1

Ready in: 15 minutes, plus 10 minutes marinating time

1 × 150g (5 oz) boneless, skinless
   salmon fillet, cut into 2.5cm (1 inch)
   cubes
2 spring onions (green onions), sliced
½ red pepper, cubed
5 tenderstem broccoli (broccolini)
   tips
2 tsp sesame seeds

For the marinade:
1 tbsp dark soy sauce
2 tsp mirin or rice wine vinegar
2 tsp honey
1 clove of garlic, crushed
1 tsp freshly grated ginger

To serve:
noodles or rice

1. In a shallow dish, mix together all the marinade ingredients, then add the salmon, turn to coat and leave to marinate for 10 minutes.

2. Preheat the air fryer to 190°C (375°F). Place the vegetables in the bottom of a metal cake tin or ovenproof dish. Place the salmon on top and drizzle over the marinade. Place in the air fryer and cook for 8 minutes, stirring gently halfway through to coat the vegetables in the sauce, until the salmon is cooked and the vegetables are tender.

3. Serve immediately with noodles or rice, pouring any sauce from the tin over the vegetables and fish and sprinkling with sesame seeds.

KOREAN CHICKEN WINGS WITH KIMCHI DIP

Serves: 1
Ready in: 15 minutes

4 chicken wings

For the sauce:
2 tsp rice wine vinegar
1 tsp honey
1 tsp dark soy sauce
½ tsp garlic paste
1 tsp ginger paste
1 tsp sesame oil
1 tsp gochujang (Korean red pepper paste)

For the kimchi dip:
2 tbsp kimchi
2 tbsp fat-free Greek yogurt
2 tsp lemon juice

To serve:
1 tsp sesame seeds
1 spring onion (green onion), thinly sliced

1. Mix together all the sauce ingredients in a bowl and add the chicken wings. Stir well to coat the wings in the sauce.

2. Preheat the air fryer to 200°C (400°F). Place the chicken wings in a single layer in the air fryer and cook for 8 minutes, basting with the sauce halfway through. Turn the chicken over, brush with sauce again and cook for a further 5 minutes until the chicken is cooked and the skin is crispy.

3. Meanwhile, stir together all the ingredients for the dip in a bowl until well combined.

4. Place the wings in a shallow bowl and scatter over the sesame seeds and spring onions (green onions). Serve immediately with the kimchi dip.

KATSU SWEET POTATO CURRY

Serves: 1

Ready in: 20 minutes

125g (4½ oz) sweet potato, peeled
   and cut on the diagonal into 4–5
   slices about 1cm (¼ inch) thick
2 tbsp plain flour
2 tbsp cold water
25g (¼ cup) panko breadcrumbs
sunflower oil, for spritzing

For the sauce:
1 tsp vegetable or sunflower oil
½ small onion, finely chopped
½ tsp garlic paste
1 tsp ginger paste
½ carrot, peeled and diced
2 tsp mild curry powder
1 tsp plain flour
200ml (¾ cup) hot vegetable stock
1 tsp light soy sauce
1 tsp jarred apple sauce
salt and freshly ground black pepper

To serve:
basmati rice

1. To make the katsu sauce, heat the oil in a pan, add the onion, garlic paste and ginger paste and cook for 2 minutes, then stir in the carrots. Cover and cook over a low heat for 8 minutes, stirring occasionally, until the vegetables have softened and are starting to caramelize.

2. Stir in the curry powder and flour and cook for 2 minutes, then gradually stir in the stock, soy sauce and apple sauce. Reduce the heat, cover and simmer for 6 minutes. Season to taste. Press the sauce through a sieve (strainer).

3. For the sweet potato slices, place the flour in a small bowl and stir in the water to make a smooth, thick paste, then season. Place the breadcrumbs on a plate. Dip each slice of sweet potato first in the paste and then in the breadcrumbs to coat.

4. Preheat the air fryer to 180°C (350°F). Place the potato slices in a single layer in the air fryer, spritz with a little oil and cook for 18–20 minutes, turning halfway through and spritzing with a little more oil until the potato is tender and crisp on the outside.

5. Serve the potato slices immediately with the curry sauce and rice.

VEGETABLE AND TOFU PAD THAI

Serves: 1
Ready in: about 12 minutes

50g (2 oz) dried flat rice noodles
100g (3½ oz) extra firm tofu, cut into
  small cubes
sunflower oil, for spritzing
½ red pepper, thinly sliced
½ carrot, peeled and cut into thin
  strips
100g (3½ oz) fresh beansprouts
4 spring onions (green onions), cut
  on the diagonal

For the pad thai sauce:
1 tbsp tamarind paste
1 tbsp light soy sauce
1 tbsp siracha chilli sauce
1 tbsp vegan fish sauce
1 tbsp vegan oyster sauce
juice ½ lime
1 tsp soft brown sugar

To serve:
2 tbsp roasted peanuts, roughly
  chopped
a few slices of red chilli
1 lime wedge

1. Place the noodles in a large bowl and pour over boiling water to cover. Allow to soak for about 4–5 minutes or according to package instructions, stirring once to separate the noodles, until tender. Drain well.

2. Preheat the air fryer to 180°C (350°F). Place the tofu in the air fryer, spritz with a little oil and cook for 4 minutes. Shake the tofu, add the red pepper and carrot, spritz with a little more oil and cook for a further 2 minutes. Add the beansprouts and spring onions (green onions), stir well and cook for another 2 minutes.

3. In a small bowl, mix together all the sauce ingredients.

4. Tip the tofu and vegetables into the bottom of the air fryer, removing the rack. Add the noodles, pour over the sauce and toss to coat. Cook for a further 2–3 minutes until the sauce has heated through.

5. Transfer to a bowl. Top with a few slices of chilli, scatter with peanuts and serve with the lime wedge to squeeze over.

FAKEAWAYS

MISO-GLAZED AUBERGINE WITH SESAME SPINACH

Serves: 1
Ready in: about 20 minutes

½ aubergine (eggplant), cut into 4–5 rounds about 1.5cm (¾ inch) thick and scored with criss-cross lines on one side (being careful not to cut all the way through)

1 tbsp white miso paste

1 tbsp rice wine vinegar or mirin

1 tbsp sake or water

1 tsp dark soy sauce

1 tsp caster sugar

sunflower oil, for spritzing

100g (3½ oz) fresh baby spinach

½ tsp toasted sesame oil

To serve:

1 tsp toasted black and white sesame seeds

1 small spring onion (green onion), thinly sliced

steamed jasmine rice

1. Mix together the miso paste, rice wine, sake or water, soy sauce and sugar in a bowl.

2. Add the aubergine (eggplant), turn to coat in the sauce, then leave for 5 minutes to absorb the flavours.

3. Preheat the air fryer to 180°C (350°F). Place the aubergine unscored side down on an air-fryer liner or a piece of pierced non-stick baking (parchment) paper in the air fryer. Spoon over a little sauce from the bowl, spritz with a little oil and cook for 7 minutes. Turn over and spoon over more of the sauce, spritz with a little more oil and cook for a further 6–7 minutes until soft and slightly caramelized.

4. Transfer to a serving dish, remove the air-fryer rack and place the spinach in the bottom of the basket. Add 1 teaspoon boiling water and cook for 1 minute. Drizzle over the sesame oil, stir well, then cook for another minute until wilted.

5. Serve the aubergine with the sesame spinach and jasmine rice, sprinkled with the sesame seeds and spring onions (green onions).

PANEER, POTATO AND PEA CURRY

Serves: 1

Ready in: about 18 minutes

1 tsp sunflower oil, divided, plus extra
   for spritzing
½ small onion, finely chopped
½ tsp garlic paste
1 tsp ginger paste
1 small potato, peeled and cut into
   1cm (¼ inch) cubes
100g (3 oz) paneer cheese, cut into
   1.5cm (¾ inch) cubes
1 tsp ground coriander
1 tsp garam masala
½ tsp cumin seeds
¼ tsp ground turmeric
salt and freshly ground black pepper
1–2 small green chillies, halved
   lengthways
6 curry leaves
2 large ripe tomatoes, finely
   chopped
25g (¼ cup) frozen peas
a splash of boiling water

To serve:
mini naan bread

1. Preheat the air fryer to 180°C (350°F). Place half a teaspoon of the oil in the bottom of a metal cake tin and heat in the air fryer for 1 minute. Stir in the onion, garlic and ginger paste and cook for 2 minutes.

2. Meanwhile, place the potato and paneer in a bowl, add the spices, season and drizzle over the remaining oil. Shake to coat the potato in the spices.

3. Add the paneer and potato to the onions along with the chilli and curry leaves, stir well and cook for 8 minutes, stirring gently halfway through.

4. Add the tomatoes, peas and boiling water and stir, then cook for 3–4 minutes.

5. Transfer to a bowl and serve with naan bread on the side.

DONER KEBAB WITH FLATBREAD

Serves: 1
Ready in: 35 minutes

For the kebab:
150g (5 oz) 10%-fat lamb mince
  (ground lamb)
½ onion, coarsely grated
1 clove of garlic, crushed
½ tsp ground cumin
½ tsp ground coriander
½ tsp smoked paprika
½ tsp oregano
salt and freshly ground black pepper
sunflower oil, for brushing

For the flatbread:
50g (¼ cup) self-raising flour, plus
  extra for dusting (see tip on
  page 20)
a pinch of salt
50g (¼ cup) natural yogurt
olive oil, for spritzing

**To serve (in any combination
  you prefer):**
chopped tomato
chilli sauce
tzatziki
shredded red or white cabbage
thinly sliced red onion
thinly sliced pickled peppers

1. To make the kebab, place all the ingredients in a food processor and pulse until everything is combined. Remove and shape into a thick sausage.

2. Brush a piece of foil with the oil, then add the sausage mixture and roll up to fully encase, twisting the ends of the foil.

3. Preheat the air fryer to 180°C (350°F). Place the foil-wrapped kebab in the air fryer and cook for 20 minutes, turning halfway through. Remove the foil, increase the temperature to 200°C (400°F) and cook for a further 6–8 minutes, turning once until browned. Remove. Cover with foil and leave to rest for 5 minutes.

4. Meanwhile, place the flour, salt and yogurt in a bowl. Mix the ingredients to form a rough dough. Lightly dust the worktop with a little flour, then knead the mixture for 1–2 minutes until the dough is smooth. Roll out into an oval shape, about 12cm (5 inches) wide.

5. Spritz with a little oil, cook at 200°C (400°F) for 6 minutes until golden brown and slightly puffed. Thinly slice the meat.

6. Split the flatbread, fill with the meat and your choice of accompaniments.

PULLED MUSHROOM TACOS

Serves: 1
Ready in: 20 minutes

For the pickled radishes and onions:
3 radishes, thinly sliced
3 thinly sliced red onion rings, halved
juice ½ lime
a pinch of salt

For the mashed avocado:
1 ripe baby avocado, peeled, stoned
   and chopped
juice ½ lime
1 tbsp fresh coriander (cilantro),
   chopped
salt and freshly ground black pepper

For the mushrooms:
125g (4 oz) king oyster mushrooms
1 tsp sunflower oil
½ small onion, chopped
1 clove garlic, crushed
½ tsp ground cumin
½ tsp smoked paprika
1–2 tsp chipotle chilli paste (adobo
   sauce)
1 tbsp dark soy sauce
1 tbsp maple syrup
1 tsp tomato purée (tomato paste)

To serve:
2–3 small soft taco wraps (tortillas)
shredded lettuce

1. Place the radishes and onions in a bowl, then add the lime juice and a pinch of salt. Mix and leave to stand.

2. Place the avocado in a bowl. Add the lime juice and coriander (cilantro), mash together with a fork and season to taste.

3. To prepare the mushrooms, cut off the caps and slice these into thin strips, then shred the stems with a fork by scoring the length of the body. Turn each mushroom and work around it, then tear the shredded mushroom into long pieces.

4. Preheat the air fryer to 180°C (350°F). Place the oil in an ovenproof dish or metal cake tin, then add the onion, garlic and dry spices and turn to coat. Place in the air fryer and cook for 2 minutes, stirring halfway through.

5. Meanwhile, mix together the chilli paste, soy sauce, maple syrup and tomato purée (tomato paste) in a large bowl. Stir in the mushrooms to coat. Add to the onion mix, stir and cook in the air fryer for 8 minutes, stirring halfway through.

6. To serve, warm the wraps (tortillas), add some lettuce and top with the mushrooms, pickles and avocado.

FAKEAWAYS

SOUTHERN AIR-FRIED CHICKEN WITH CORN ON THE COB

Serves: 1

Ready in: about 35 minutes, plus 10 minutes marinating time

4 tbsp buttermilk or natural yogurt
1 tsp hot chilli sauce
2 bone-in, skin-on chicken thighs
salt and freshly ground black pepper

For the coating:
3 tbsp plain flour
1 tbsp cornflour (cornstarch)
½ tsp garlic powder
½ tsp onion powder
1 tsp smoked paprika
1 tsp ground black pepper
1 tsp dried mixed herbs
½ tsp salt

1 corn on the cob, husk and silk
   removed
1 tbsp melted butter

To serve:
coleslaw

1. Place the buttermilk in a bowl, stir in the chilli sauce and seasoning. Add the chicken pieces, stir to coat and leave to one side for 10 minutes.

2. In another bowl, combine all the ingredients for the coating, making sure they are well mixed.

3. Stand the corn upright on a chopping board and using a sharp knife and a rocking movement cut in half lengthways, then cut each in half again so you have 4 corn ribs. Brush all over with the melted butter and season well.

4. Dip each piece of chicken in the flour mixture until fully coated, shaking off any excess. Place on plate for 5 minutes. (This ensures the coating sticks to the chicken.)

5. Preheat the air fryer to 180°C (350°F), spritz the chicken all over with oil and cook for 15 minutes, turn, spritz with more oil and add the buttered sweetcorn. Cook for another 10–12 minutes until the chicken is golden, crisp and cooked through and the corn is tender and slightly charred.

6. Serve with coleslaw.

FAKEAWAYS

SWEET TREATS

BERRY OATY CRUMBLE

Serves: 1
Ready in: 10 minutes

125g (4 oz) mixed frozen berries
1 tsp soft brown sugar
1 tsp cornflour (cornstarch)

For the crumble topping:
4 tbsp whole rolled porridge oats
   (old-fashioned rolled oats)
1 tsp soft brown sugar
1 tsp melted coconut oil or butter
¼ tsp ground ginger or cinnamon

To serve:
vanilla ice cream or custard

1. Preheat the air fryer to 180°C (350°F). Place the berries in a 250ml (1 cup) ovenproof dish and stir in the sugar and cornflour (cornstarch). Place the dish in the air fryer and cook for 3 minutes, then stir well.

2. Meanwhile, place the oats in a small bowl and stir in all the remaining crumble topping ingredients. Spoon the crumble over the berries, return the dish to the air fryer and cook for 8–10 minutes until golden and bubbling.

3. Serve warm with ice cream or custard.

COCONUT, CHILLI AND LIME PINEAPPLE FINGERS

Serves: 1
Ready in: 15 minutes, plus 10 minutes marinating time

1 tsp soft brown sugar
finely grated zest and juice ½ lime
1 Thai red chilli, deseeded and finely chopped
freshly ground black pepper
3 pineapple fingers (spears)
1 tbsp desiccated coconut (dried coconut)

1. Mix together the sugar, lime zest and juice, and the chilli in a bowl with a good grind of black pepper. Add the pineapple fingers (spears), stir to coat, then leave to marinate for 10 minutes.

2. Preheat the air fryer to 180°C (350°F). Place the pineapple fingers inside in a single layer on an air-fryer liner or piece of pierced non-stick baking (parchment) paper. Cook for 12 minutes, turning halfway through and basting with any remaining mixture from the bowl until slightly caramelized. Sprinkle with the coconut and cook for a further 3 minutes until the coconut is lightly toasted.

3. Serve warm, drizzled with any juices from the air fryer and your choice of ice cream or custard.

CHOCOLATE AND PISTACHIO BROWNIE

Serves: 1
Ready in: 10 minutes

sunflower oil or baking spray
  for greasing
2 tbsp plain flour
1 tbsp soft brown sugar
1 tbsp cocoa powder
½ tsp vanilla extract
1 tbsp olive or sunflower oil
2 tbsp milk
1 tbsp chopped pistachios
1 tsp dark chocolate chips

To serve:
pistachio or vanilla ice cream

This delicious brownie is slightly gooey on the inside. You can substitute the pistachios for any chopped nuts.

1. Lightly grease a 150ml (⅔ cup) ramekin or small cake tin. Mix together the flour, sugar and cocoa powder in a small bowl, then stir in the oil, vanilla extract and milk to form a smooth batter with no lumps. Stir in the nuts and the chocolate chips.

2. Preheat the air fryer to 160°C (325°F). Add the mixture to the prepared dish and cook in the air fryer for 9 minutes.

3. Serve warm with a scoop of your chosen ice cream.

BAKED ALMOND AND CINNAMON APPLE RINGS

Serves: 1
Ready in: 14 minutes

2 tbsp ground almonds
½ tsp ground cinnamon
1 eating apple, cored and cut into
   1cm (¼ inch) rings
1 tsp melted coconut oil

To serve:
fresh raspberries
Greek or plant-based natural yogurt

1. Mix together the almonds and cinnamon on a small plate. Brush both sides of each apple ring with the oil and then press both sides into the almond mixture to coat.

2. Preheat the air fryer to 190°C (375°F). Place the apple rings in a single layer in the air fryer and cook for 12 minutes, turning halfway through until the crumb is crisp and the apple tender.

3. Serve in a stack with raspberries and yogurt.

PEACHES WITH HONEY AND THYME

Serves: 1
Ready in: 12 minutes

1 tsp honey
¼ tsp vanilla extract
½ tsp fresh lemon thyme leaves
1 peach, not too ripe, stoned and halved

To serve:
natural yogurt
toasted hazelnuts, chopped

1. Mix together the honey, vanilla extract and thyme in a bowl. Add the peach halves, cut-side down, and coat in the honey.

2. Preheat the air fryer to 180°C (350°F). Place the peach halves inside, cut-side up, on an air-fryer liner or piece of pierced non-stick baking (parchment) paper. Drizzle over any remaining honey mixture from the bowl and cook for 10–12 minutes until tender and lightly caramelized.

3. Serve with a spoonful of yogurt, scattered with chopped hazelnuts.

STICKY BAKED FIGS WITH ROSEWATER YOGURT

|||||||||||||||||||||||||||||||||||||||||||||||||||||||||||||||||||||||||||||||||||||||||||||||||||||||||||||||||

Serves: 1
Ready in: 8 minutes

2 medium figs
½ tbsp butter
1 tsp honey
¼ tsp ground mixed spice (pumpkin
   pie spice)

For the rosewater and honey yogurt:
2 tbsp fat-free Greek yogurt
1 tsp honey
¼ tsp rosewater, or to taste

1. Cut a deep cross in the top of each fig then ease the top apart like a flower. Sit the figs in a small ovenproof baking dish and add a small piece of the butter into the centre of each fig. Drizzle the honey over the figs, then sprinkle with the mixed spice.

2. Preheat the air fryer to 190°C (375°F). Place the dish inside and cook for 6 minutes until the figs are softened and the sauce is sticky.

3. Meanwhile, mix together all the ingredients for the rosewater yogurt in a small bowl.

4. Serve the figs warm with the yogurt.

MAPLE AND PECAN CARAMELIZED BANANA

Serves: 1
Ready in: 7 minutes

1 tsp melted butter or plant-based
   butter
1 tsp maple syrup
1 firm banana, halved lengthways
2 tsp pecans, chopped

To serve:
coconut yogurt

1. In a small dish, mix together the butter and maple syrup. Brush the cut side of the banana halves with half the mixture.

2. Preheat the air fryer to 190°C (375°F). Place the banana halves inside, cut-side down, on an air-fryer liner or piece of pierced non-stick baking (parchment) paper. Brush with the remaining butter mixture and cook for 5 minutes. Carefully turn over, sprinkle over the nuts and cook for a further 2 minutes.

3. Transfer to a plate and pour over any sauce from the air fryer. Serve immediately with a spoonful of coconut yogurt.

GOOEY CHOCOLATE AND COFFEE PUDDING

Serves: 1
Ready in: 10 minutes

1 tbsp butter, plus extra for greasing
25g (1 oz) 70% cocoa dark chocolate,
  broken into pieces
2 tsp icing sugar (powdered sugar)
1 tbsp plain flour
2 tsp instant espresso powder,
  dissolved in 2 tsp boiling water
2 tbsp milk

To serve:
vanilla ice cream or crème fraîche
fresh raspberries

1. Preheat the air fryer to 75°C (165°F). Grease a 150ml (⅔ cup) metal pudding tin or ramekin with butter. Place the chocolate in a small bowl with the rest of the butter. Place the bowl in the air fryer and heat for 3 minutes, stirring once, until the chocolate and butter have melted. Allow to cool slightly.

2. Preheat the air fryer to 190°C (375°F). Stir the sugar, flour, espresso powder and milk into the chocolate and spoon the mixture into the prepared tin. Place in the air fryer and cook for 5 minutes until the outside is cooked and the centre is molten. Place a plate over the top and invert onto a small plate.

3. Serve immediately with a scoop of ice cream or crème fraiche and raspberries.

LEMON PAVLOVA WITH STRAWBERRIES

Serves: 1
Ready in: 45 minutes, plus cooling time

For the meringue:
1 egg white
50g (¼ cup) caster sugar
¼ tsp cornflour (cornstarch)
¼ tsp white wine vinegar
finely grated zest of 1 lemon

For the filling:
3 tbsp fat-free Greek yogurt
1–2 tsp lemon curd, to taste
4–5 strawberries, sliced

To serve:
1 tsp toasted flaked almonds

1. Place the egg white into a clean mixing bowl and use an electric whisk to beat into stiff peaks. Add the sugar a teaspoon at a time, whisking well after each addition until the mixture is smooth, thick and glossy. Whisk in the cornflour (cornstarch) and vinegar and stir in the lemon zest.

2. Spoon the mixture into a 12–13cm circle on an air-fryer liner or piece of pierced non-stick baking (parchment) paper. Using the back of a spoon, make a dip in the centre of the meringue.

3. Preheat the air fryer to 120°C (250°F). Place the meringue, still on the liner, inside and cook for 35–40 minutes until the outside is dry and firm. Allow to cool in the air fryer, as the meringue will continue to crisp up.

4. Place the yogurt and lemon curd in a bowl and stir to mix. Spoon into the centre of the cooled meringue, top with the strawberries and serve immediately sprinkled with the flaked almonds.

INDEX